W9-BLE-335

Remembering Patsy

BRIAN MANSFIELD

RUTLEDGE HILL PRESS™

Nashville, Tennessee

A DIVISION OF THOMAS NELSON, INC.

www.ThomasNelson.com

Copyright © 2002 by Rutledge Hill Press.

All rights reserved.
No portion of this book may be reproduced, stored in a retrieval system,
or transmitted in any form or by any means—electronic, mechanical, photocopy,
recording, or any other—except for brief quotations in printed reviews,
without prior permission of the publisher.

Published by Rutledge Hill Press,
a division of Thomas Nelson, Inc., P.O. Box 141000, Nashville, Tennessee 37214.

Photo Credits
Photos by Les Leverett: pages ii, 21, 25, 27, 29, 31, 33, 45, 47,
55, 59, 61, 63, 67, 69, 73, 75, 77, 81, 85, 87, 89, 91, 93, 95.
Photos courtesy of Country Music Hall of Fame:
pages 11, 15, 19, 23, 35, 37, 39, 41, 43, 65, 71, 79.
Photos courtesy of Grand Ole Opry Museum: pages 13, 17, 49, 51, 53, 57, 83.

Book design by Bruce Gore / Gore Studio, Inc.

Library of Congress Cataloging-in-Publication Data
Mansfield, Brian, 1963–
Remembering Patsy / Brian Mansfield.
    p. cm.
ISBN 1-40160-033-6
   1. Cline, Patsy, 1932–1963. 2. Country musicians—United
States—Biography. I. Title.
ML420.C57 M36 2002
782.421642'092—dc21

2002011367

Printed in the United States of America

02 03 04 05 06 — 5 4 3 2 1

To them, she was just Patsy.

She was the saucy, strong-willed brunette from Virginia with the voice that could do almost anything. They admired her straightforwardness, her vitality, and her raw sensuality. She had a great big grin framed by full red lips, and she liked to tease and to call people "hoss" or "chief." To them, Patsy "gave as good as she got" and "didn't take nothing from nobody." Ask them and they will tell you that Patsy was a woman "who would tell you like it was." She was her own person. She was a wife and a mother of two young children, Julie and Randy. She was a fellow performer. She was a friend.

If they had known she was going to be gone so soon, they would've paid closer attention and tried harder to commit those days to memory. They would've cherished each mundane moment, each wisecrack, each friendly jab, each time the curtain of her tough exterior blew back to offer a glimpse of the vulnerable woman it concealed. They would've taken more pictures, run tape on more interviews. They would've recorded her more.

But who had any idea what would happen? Although Patsy joked recklessly about her own death after a terrifying close call in a 1961 car wreck, nobody ever imagined that on March 5, 1963, as Patsy, manager Randy Hughes, and fellow singers Cowboy Copas and Hawkshaw Hawkins flew back from a benefit concert for the family of a Kansas City disc jockey, Hughes's single-engine Piper Comanche 250 would crash near Camden, Tennessee, killing all aboard.

Patsy made her reputation in a tragically brief time. "Walkin' after Midnight," her first hit, came in 1957. The rest of her best-known songs—"I Fall to Pieces," "Crazy," "She's Got You," "Sweet Dreams (of You)," and

"Faded Love" among them—all came between 1961 and 1963. During just two years, Patsy Cline forever changed country music. She has sold more than twenty-five million records. Perhaps only Hank Williams, who also died too young, matches her for influence on future generations of singers.

If Patsy had lived, who knows how things might have been different? By most accounts, Patsy was just coming into her own as an entertainer. Her producer, Owen Bradley, was just getting her to share the vision he had for her, a vision that encompassed not only the realm of country music but a broader-based audience as well. Three of the singles Patsy released in 1961 and 1962 climbed both the country and the pop charts. She was beginning to shed her cowgirl costumes for more formal stage gowns.

Patsy might've gone on to stardom in both the country and pop worlds like Brenda Lee, also part of Bradley's Decca Records fold. Perhaps she would've been wiped away in the wake of the Beatles' arrival in America. Given her generous spirit, she likely would have assumed the role of Nashville matriarch, offering advice and assistance to up-and-coming singers like Dottie West, Loretta Lynn, Tammy Wynette, and Dolly Parton, and later Trisha Yearwood, k.d. lang, Patty Loveless, even Shania Twain. On the other hand, her sharp tongue and complete lack of interest in people she didn't like might've shortened her stay at the top. Part of the fascination with Patsy comes from expectations unfulfilled.

The people who knew Patsy personally have begun to leave, too. Dottie West, her friend. Owen Bradley, her producer. Harlan Howard, who helped write songs like "I Fall to Pieces." There is a photograph in this book of Patsy disembarking from an airplane in triumphant arrival for a concert at New York City's Carnegie Hall. She's surrounded by Minnie

Pearl, Jim Reeves, Faron Young, Bill Monroe, and Grandpa Jones. Every one of them is gone now; not all of them died young.

Of those who remain, some feel like they've shared every thought, every private moment, so the rest of us can know her better. Some have said all they want. Some still get tears in their eyes when they think about her, about what happened and what might've been.

Most of us, though, know Patsy only from her recordings, from the photographs, from the occasional video clip from *Arthur Godfrey's Talent Scouts*. We imagine her from Beverly D'Angelo's portrayal in the Loretta Lynn biopic *Coal Miner's Daughter* and from Jessica Lange's Oscar-nominated performance in 1985's *Sweet Dreams*, the film that transformed Patsy from Nashville treasure into revered international icon. We recognize her from the catch in her voice and for the dramatic flourishes that she favored to finish songs like "Walkin' after Midnight" and "Leavin' on Your Mind." Now, like James Dean or Marilyn Monroe, she represents both eternal youth and youth cut short, with lively eyes that haunt us from black-and-white photographs.

Those who knew Patsy just as Patsy now know her as so much more. But they, like us, are left with these little things. They have the pictures, the records. They've also got their memories.

And they remember.

ACKNOWLEDGMENTS

WHEN YOU ASK Patsy Cline's friends to talk about her, you get basically two responses. There are the ones who feel their memories have been picked clean already, and they don't want to say any more. Then there are others who feel their memories have been picked clean already, and they don't know what more they could possibly say. I want to express my deepest gratitude to those people who shared, once again, their most bittersweet reminiscences, particularly Jan Howard, Charlie Dick, Dale Turner Westberry, Bill Anderson, Billy Walker, Hank Cochran, George Hamilton IV, Jim Ed Brown, Gordon Stoker, and Ray Walker.

Thanks also to those who made introductions, offered assistance, and provided direction: Jessie Schmidt, Darlene Bieber, Paul Kingsbury, Harold Bradley, Schatzi Hageman, Jenni Bohler, Storme Warren, Greg Travis, Kirt Webster, Martha Moore, Nancy Russell, and Scott Stem. Photographer Les Leverett showed me a new way to look at the past, and Bryan Curtis at Rutledge Hill gave me the chance to put it into words.

Finally, there are three people without whose patience and forbearance I would not have been able to complete this book: John Bitzer and Ken Barnes, two of my editors; and my lovely wife, Nancy.

Remembering Patsy

Dale Turner Westberry

FRIEND

SHE HAD CUT some records by the time I
met her, but they were the early ones.
You already knew Patsy was a star, even if
the rest of the world didn't. . . . She just
stood out. That voice was unusual. Her
showmanship for that time was unusual.
She had flair. Most of us just sang a song,
but she could put it over.

Charlie Dick

HUSBAND

I WAS JUST looking for somebody to dance
with. I guess there was probably a little ego
there, saying, "She's up there on stage.
She's somebody. Let's see if I can dance with
her." Playing games, I guess. . . . I had
another girlfriend at that time who was at
that dance. She wasn't with me, but she
was there. Then she got involved, and it
got funny. Patsy told her to go away. That
made me feel good, because I was trying
to make the other one jealous, I don't
know. Anyhow, I just thought she was
about as crazy as I was, and we was going
to have a lot of fun.

Charlie Dick

SHE SAID, and I guess it's true, that one night, we were talking about something, and I said, "After we get married, we're going to do this." She said, "Oh, we're going to get married?" I said, "Hell, I guess so." That was it. At least that's what she told me.

Roger Miller

She liked to come to Tootsie's with Charlie. We'd have a few beers, laugh, and play music. We usually would wind up at somebody's house after Tootsie's closed. It would close around midnight. Then we'd go out to somebody's house and sing all night. We had some great times and made some good memories.

She loved to laugh. She told a lot of dirty jokes. She liked to howl and laugh. She had a good soul and a good heart. She was a really good person, a person you wanted to have in your corner.

Charlie Dick

THE BIGGEST single date she ever played was $1,200. It was in Ozark, Alabama. When they called to book the show, Randy, her agent, said, "Who else is on the show?" Well, it was Bobby Vee and Roy Orbison. He said, "Well, hell, this is not a country show, it's a rock show. They get more money than hillbillies do." So he jacked her price up.

Patty Griffin

WHAT I GATHER from listening to her sing is that she had a personal elegance about her and was very secure in that. Since I know a little bit about growing up poor, I think it's an incredible beauty. It's like a really elegant wildflower. That's how I think of her voice.

Willie Nelson

I MET PATSY pretty early. I met her husband, Charlie Dick, in Tootsie's across the street from the Grand Ole Opry one night when I first came to town. I met her then. I was playing bass with Ray Price, so we worked a few towns where she played on the bill with us. I knew her well enough to say hello. She recorded "Crazy," and I got to know her a little better after that. She was already road-wise. She'd been there and done that. She was one of those strong-willed persons, and she had the greatest voice.

Trisha Yearwood

IT'S A *big* voice. It's not a wimpy voice. It's not thin—ever. It's just *big*. The other thing about it is that it is very emotional. You hear the breath. It's like she's standing in the room with you, singing. You hear her voice catch, the little lick that she does.... There's a magic about a few artists—she's one of them, Elvis is one—they have something in their voices that just mesmerizes you. That's the way her voice was for me. And is, still, for me.

Loretta Lynn

SHE ALWAYS bought me stuff. Because I didn't have nothin', not even panties. She give me a pair of panties—and this is no lie—they were hand-me-downs, because she'd wore 'em forever, too. You know, them dadgum panties, I don't know what I did with them, but they like to have never worn out. I wore 'em for three or four years. Oh, I'd take 'em off and wash 'em, put 'em back on. Them were darn good panties. I'd like to get some more of them.

Jan Howard

I MET HER at the Opry when I first came there.... I was very shy. I wouldn't go up and introduce myself to anyone, and I wouldn't hang around.

It was the women's restroom, our dressing room.... She'd finished singing, and I'd gone back to change clothes. She opened the door and just kind of stood there with her hands on her hips.... She said, "Well, you're a conceited little son of a bitch." I said, "What?" She said, "Well, you just waltz in here and do your bit and then waltz out. You don't say hello, kiss my ass, or anything else to anybody."

Then my Irish and Indian temper came to the surface. I said, "Now, wait just a damn minute. Where I'm from, it's the people that live there that make a stranger feel welcome and not a damn soul made me feel welcome here." And she just rared back and laughed. She said, "You're all right, honey. Anybody that'll talk back to the Cline is all right." She called herself "the Cline." She said, "We're going to be good friends." And we were.

k.d. lang

ON MY twenty-first birthday, I was given
two Patsy Cline albums, because it was
post—*Coal Miner's Daughter*.... I started
listening to them seriously and just being
blown away by her interpretive quality and
the timbre of her voice.... It was pretty
powerful stuff, powerful to the point
where it was transforming.

Brenda Lee

I REMEMBER she had a great figure. She just looked great in her clothes. The kind of figure that turned men's eyes. She really was built up.

Minnie Pearl

I THINK her wardrobe had a lot to do with
her being known as a sex symbol. She wore
tight clothes. Tight around her hips. Flashy
material. She went in for sequins and lamé,
gold and silver lamé. And she went in for a
little shorter dresses than most of those
girls were wearing at that point. Patsy stuck
to shirtwaist type dresses, but very tight.
And she could wear 'em. She knew how to
wear 'em. And high-heeled shoes. It kind
of went with her. I mean, it was the pack-
age. She had a full figure: she was not over-
weight. I just think she was a big girl. She
was a sexy girl. I would like to see her walk
out and compete with some of these girls
now. I've seen some television stuff that
they've unearthed. It doesn't do her justice.

PATSY WITH FERLIN HUSKY.

Gordon Stoker

THE JORDANAIRES

SHE CALLED everybody "hoss." That was her nice word. She had some pretty dirty words she used a lot of times. She was very plainspoken. Patsy was about the only person we worked with, I guess, that really let you know what side of the fence you were on.

Bill Anderson

SHE WAS one of the boys. She was just one of the guys. You didn't have to watch anything you said or did around her, because chances are she said or did it first.

PATSY WITH MARTY SALKIN AND PAUL COHEN OF DECCA RECORDS.

Ray Walker

WHEN OWEN first tried to get her to sing a ballad, she was scared to death. On "I Fall to Pieces," at the end of that she started to do a Western-swing ending. We looked stunned. My jaw dropped. She walked over to me and she said, "What's the matter, hoss? Did you like that?" I said, "Well, do you want me to say?" She said, "Yeah, spit it out." I said, "Patsy, you had us in the palm of your hand, but that tag, it ruined the song for me." She said, "That's what Owen thought. Owen thought I ought to leave it like a ballad." I said, "Honey, trust Owen. Owen knows exactly what the song needs, and he knows what you can do. Go on down there and get those low notes you got." That was one of our first encounters with her.

Amy Grant

I WAS DOING a show one time out at the
Opry House. I was sharing a dressing room
with Loretta Lynn and probably about
forty other women. I was trying to kind of
spice up my outfit a little bit. Loretta came
over and said, "Hey, let me show you
something Patsy used to do." I had some
clip-on earrings, and she pulled my earrings off and said, "Hey, just clip 'em on
your shoes." It won't be long and nobody
will be able to say, "We used to do it this
way." It'll just be us remembering.

Ralph Emery

I WAS THE all-night disc jockey at WSM. I had a
lot of drop-ins by various stars, with their records
or just to come and chat. Besides, I was open later
than Tootsie's Orchid Lounge.

Patsy Cline, who loved to party, would come
by the show at night. . . . She'd come in with
Charlie and three or four other people. The
party sort of still would be going on, even
though they were in the studio. I really wasn't
sure why they came by, except to say hello. But
if I tried to do any interviewing, it really wasn't
working, because they had, apparently, some
inside jokes going. . . .

But one night she came in by herself.
I thought, "This is great. Perhaps we can get
something done tonight." And we did. If I had
had the good sense to know that Patsy Cline
was going to be such an icon, I would have
rolled tape on that interview.

Grant Turner

OPRY ANNOUNCER

WE DID A lot of commercials there in the WSM studio. So they called her in and several other people that were going to be on, and while we were waiting to get set up—whenever you're doing anything of that nature, there are always a certain number of delays—she had brought all her bills with her and her checkbook and she was writing out checks to pay her bills during the time we were waiting. And I thought, she knows how to make good use of all her time, because she is so busy traveling and appearing here and there. And she didn't have an office, she didn't have a secretary. There she was, writing her own checks while we were all setting up there.

PATSY WITH DISC JOCKEY LORIN HARRISON.

Ray Walker

THE JORDANAIRES

PATSY WAS a true-blue person, fiery as she could be if she needed to be. But she always had a good heart for what was right. I guess she treated herself worse than she treated anybody else.

PATSY WITH RANDY HUGHES.

Loretta Lynn

I GOT THE Most Up-and-Coming Female
Artist in Nashville, Tennessee, the first year
I went back there. This girl singer come
up to Patsy and said, "I wonder how many
bed sheets that Doyle Wilburn had to turn
down for her to get that?" Patsy took her
coat off, and she said, "Charlie, hold my
coat!"... She was going to whip her.
Charlie had to hold her instead of her coat.
My husband helped. And it took both of
them to do it.

George Hamilton IV

SHE LOVED to tease people. She called me "Mr. Goody Two-Shoes." She referred to me to my face as "the Pat Boone of country music." But it was always with her tongue firmly implanted in her cheek. Charlie used to tell me, "If Patsy kids you, she likes you. If she don't kid you, she don't like you." … If she didn't like a person, she didn't waste much time with them at all. She didn't bother having disagreements. She just didn't spend any time with people she didn't like.

Jan Howard

I LOVED her laugh. Her laugh came from deep. She had a deep laugh. When she laughed, she really laughed. She didn't just smile or giggle. That giggle was not Patsy. She laughed, and it was a hearty laugh.

PATSY WITH DISC JOCKEY LEROY MORRIS.

Michelle Branch

FOR A FEW years of my childhood, Patsy Cline was all I listened to. It was kind of an obsession. My dad listened to it all the time. I would always play it.

My mom and dad never had a CD player in the car. We only had a tape deck when everyone else had a CD player. The only tape we had was Patsy Cline, so that was kind of a thing—every time we got in the car, it was either the oldies radio station or Patsy Cline.

Brenda Lee

PATSY WAS like a big sister to me.... I used to go over to her house. She'd let me wear her stage costumes and play dress-up.

Patsy with disc jockey Gary Kirtow.

Jim Ed Brown

I RESPECTED HER, because she was what she was. There were no airs. I love people like that. And she was one of those people. There were no airs to Patsy. She just told it like it was, said it like it was, and she lived the way she felt and the way she was.

PATSY WITH "GOV." JIMMIE DAVIS.

Billy Walker

RANDY HUGHES and I both threatened to nail her feet to the floor. She moved around on stage all the time when she wore those little red-and-yellow cowboy clothes and boots.... Randy wanted her to stand still and sing. He finally got her into full-length dresses.

PATSY RECEIVES AN AWARD FROM CHARLIE LAMB, PUBLISHER OF *Music Reporter*.

Harold Bradley

STUDIO MUSICIAN

SHE WAS very, very serious [in the studio]. She wanted the records to be really good. She was intense about the music, so much so that she and Owen argued about the music. He always won.

Bill Anderson

I REMEMBER Patsy riding in the back seat of my car from Nashville to North Carolina one time. Cowboy Copas was with us, and Stringbean. I remember her getting so tickled she would slide off of the seat and into the floorboard of the car. When she laughed, she laughed from the top of her head to the tip of her toes. Copas was sitting in the front seat, riding shotgun. He was facing towards the backseat, and he was telling jokes and road stories and doing impressions and stuff. She would get so tickled, she would slide into the floor, and Stringbean and I would have to take her and sit her back up on the seat. Pretty soon, she'd get to laughing again, and she'd slide right back down in the floorboard of that car.

PATSY WITH JIM REEVES AND GRANDPA JONES.

Lee Ann Womack

EVERYBODY—I don't care what kind of
music you like—everybody loves Patsy.
I don't care what the age is. Even little girls
love Patsy and the records that she made.
I guess she was just that good.

Gordon Stoker

SHE WAS always wanting love and respect from the people around her. That's the reason she loved the musicians, everybody that was on the sessions. Bob Moore, Buddy Harman, Harold Bradley—all these people she loved dearly, because she felt like we were her family. The only thing that girl wanted was to be loved and for you to like what she did.

Harlan Howard

SONGWRITER, "I FALL TO PIECES"

I DO KNOW that she loved to hang out with songwriters. She would come over, after the Opry song. She would come over to Tootsie's, and she wasn't necessarily looking for me, but looking for us, which would be Willie and Hank and I and Roger Miller, Mel Tillis, Wayne Walker, Justin Tubb, all of us guys. We were all buddies. Of course, she'd do anybody's song, but we had an inside track 'cause we were there.

PATSY WITH LEROY VAN DYKE AND CHUCK OLSON,
PUBLIC RELATIONS MANAGER FOR WSM-TV.

Jan Howard

SHE WAS REAL, very real. Nothing phony about Patsy. And she loved her fans. She would correspond with them. I know that she did answer her fan mail, and she did it personally.... She was a very warm person. And if she liked you, she loved you, and if she didn't, she let you know about it real quick. It was either black or white. Nothing phony about Patsy.

PATSY WITH DISK JOCKEY TOM REEDER.

George Hamilton IV

I WAS QUITE intimidated by her. She was
not only so talented and so gifted and so
obviously much more professional than I
was. . . . I'd never met a woman with quite
that much self-assurance and power about
her. It wasn't a cockiness, it was just a self-
assured confidence. People say, what do you
think Patsy thought of you? To be honest,
I think she thought I was a bit of a wimp.

Clockwise from bottom left, GRANDPA JONES, MINNIE PEARL, JIM REEVES, FARON YOUNG, BILL MONROE, AND PATSY ARRIVE AT LaGUARDIA.

Billy Walker

ONLY PROBABLY the last few months did she realize what she was beginning to become. She was really a country singer. Even though "Walkin' after Midnight" hit in the pop field, she was still a country singer. She never tried to make pop records until Owen began to guide her that way.

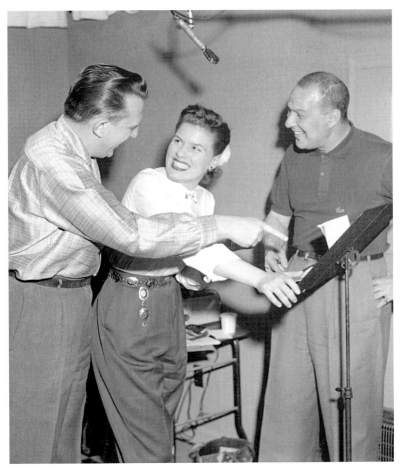

OWEN BRADLEY, PATSY, AND PAUL COHEN.

Gordon Stoker

EACH ONE of those songs that you hear her sing, that's pretty much the story of her life. She was a good person and a sweet person, but at the same time she had a lot of unlucky breaks.

Charlie Dick

A LOT OF [the film *Sweet Dreams*] was right,
but it was just way out of proportion,
where they had us actually in knock-down
drag-out fights. You might've thought that
was what was going to be, but it was more
verbal than it ever was physical. I smacked
her one time, that's a well-known story,
too, but I never *hit* her. We never had a
slugging fight like you see on TV. . . .
If you was around at the right time, you'd
think all hell was going to break loose
when we got going good. But we had a lot
of fun making up.

PATSY IN THE STUDIO WITH REX ALLEN, JUSTIN TUBB, AND ARLEIGH DUFF.

Bill Anderson

WHEN SHE finally got on that roll and finally discovered who she was as a recording artist, she had great songs. She picked great material. Patsy's voice is not dated at all. She just has that voice for all generations. . . . Owen Bradley's production on those records was just absolutely timeless production. You listen to them today and they sound just as good as they did in 1962 or '61.

Jan Howard

I WAS AT the hairdresser and Patsy was there—we went to the same hairdresser—just before they went to Kansas City. She was talking about going up there, and when they came back that she and Charlie and Randy and Kathy Hughes were going to go to the Bahamas for a few days. I said, "I hope you're not going in that rinky-dink airplane." She said, "Well, sure." I said, "Patsy, it has one engine. What are you going to do if that one engine goes out?" She said, "Ah, if the little bug goes down, I guess I'll go down with it."

Ray Walker

I WAS THE last person to see her leave the Opry. Patsy came around and hugged us all and started to leave. She had had two wrecks. She had just gotten her new, full-length coat back from the insurance company. The insurance company had replaced her mink coat. In the second wreck, right there on the wreck scene, somebody had taken that coat.

She had that coat on. She put it on after she'd hugged us all. I followed her behind the stage, toward the stage door that went down into the alley. It looked like a stone dungeon, the steps did.... I said, "Patsy, honey, be careful. We love you." She stopped. She did a half-body turn. She didn't really move her feet, she just did a half turn, twisted around, and flipped the collar of that coat up around that pretty dark hair. She had that broken tooth, you know. She looked at me, and she just glowed. Her eyes glistened. She said, "Hoss, I've had two bad ones. The next one will either be a charm or it'll kill me." Those were the last words she ever spoke at the Ryman Auditorium.

PATSY CLINE WITH LEN HENSEL, WSM SALES MANAGER.

Ralph Emery

YOU KNOW, when you're making history,
it becomes part of the job. You're on daily,
and you run into these singers. I was on the
Grand Ole Opry on the weekend. I'm sure
I introduced Patsy on a number of occa-
sions. It doesn't occur to you that these
people are going to be legends. Some wise
person said, "The gods favor those who
die young." Patsy will always be thirty years
old to all of us.

Harold Bradley

SHE'S TAKEN the standards for being a
country music vocalist, and she raised the
bar. Women, even now, are trying to get to
that bar.... If you're going to be a country
singer, if you're not going to copy her—
and most people do come to town copying
her—then you sure have to be aware of
how she did. It's always good to know what
was in the past, because you might think
you're pretty hot until you hear her....
It gives all the female singers coming in
something to gauge their talents against.
And I expect it will forever.

STANDING ON THE STEPS OF NEW YORK'S CITY HALL, GRANDPA JONES,
MINNIE PEARL, FARON YOUNG, BILL MONROE, AND PATSY
HOLD UP THEIR "KEYS TO THE CITY."

Hank Cochran

I'VE WRITTEN some songs since then, and I've just cried because she wasn't here to sing them.

I sure do miss her.